MADAME ALEXANDER
"LITTLE PEOPLE"

MADAME ALEXANDER
"LITTLE PEOPLE"

by

Marge Biggs

"To you to enjoy"
Marge Biggs

Image Printing, Sacramento, California

Published and Edited by: Marge and Cliff Biggs

Additional copies of this book may be ordered from
Marge Biggs
1311 Highridge
Riverside, CA 92506

Printed by Image Printing,
Sacramento,
California

Library of Congress
Catalog Card Number 79-66461

DEDICATION

To Madame Alexander, who gives us "The Most Beautiful Dolls in the World." To my husband Cliff, and our three sons, Tony, Shane, Joey, who share in my joys of doll collecting.

To doll lovers all over the world.

ACKNOWLEDGEMENTS

Special thanks to the following:
Cliff Biggs, my husband, for doing the article on, "Why Collect Dolls?", for assisting on the doll write-ups, and encouraging me to put the book out;

The Alexander Doll Company for the article, "Madame Alexander Begins 56th Year In Doll Business With New Line For 1979";

Bob Hug, the photographer, who dedicated many hours and lots of patience to achieve the beautiful photographs in this book;

Millie Ferguson, Marietta Lang, Tony Biggs, Shane Biggs, Joey Biggs, Marilyn Provost, Korina Provost, Georgeann Tintori, Meta Reistad, Yvonne Gadberry, Kay Gaughan, Rosy Rothschild, Teri Froehlich, Tina Ferguson, Velva Gee, Pam Temps, and Iva Lance for loaning their dolls for photographing.

CONTENTS

INTRODUCTION

DOLLS

Funk and Wagnall's Dictionary defines doll as, "A child's toy made to resemble the human figure. Collier's Encyclopedia defines doll as, "A plaything usually in the form of a baby or child, widely cherished by small girls.

WHY COLLECT DOLLS?

Ever since childhood, we have been taught to cuddle, feed, and love dolls. Now, even at an older age, it is second nature to want to possess these "little people." Madame Alexander designed and manufactured them to love, as well as to educate, so why not collect them?

Basically, each person collects their own particular kind of doll — Alexander, Barbie, Bisque, Effanbee, Vogue, or a variety of others. The trend, at present, is Madame Alexander dolls. They look human and are of the best quality. They can be reasonable or expensive. If taken care of, their value never falls. Each day, more people begin to collect them. If you are susceptible to habit, don't get started. Once you start, it's like a bee collecting honey. However, habit or hobby, it will bring you happiness, many rewarding experiences, and new acquaintances. Your entire family will become interested or involved in some way.

WHERE CAN DOLLS BE FOUND?

They can be found at toy stores, department stores, antique stores, garage sales, auctions, or etc. For example: Early one morning, my teen-age son came bursting into the house, "Mom, look what I bought!" To my surprise, it was a 10" Sound of Music doll I needed to complete my set with, marked $10.00, which he had purchased with his own money, from a near-by flea market.

MADAME ALEXANDER BEGINS 56th YEAR IN DOLL BUSINESS WITH NEW LINE FOR 1979

Four generations of practical experience and know-how regarding doll manufacture will go into the making of each Alexander Doll produced by the firm for the new line.

The Alexander Doll Company, founded by Madame Alexander in New York in 1923 had one generation of experience behind it when it was started. Madame Alexander's parents had founded the first doll hospital in the United States in 1895.

If the business philosophy of the Alexander Doll Company has followed any one theme through these many years, it has been a deep desire to obtain the best materials and put them together artistically and to create a doll of the highest quality in every way.

The first dolls produced by the newly founded Alexander Doll Company were cloth dolls with dimensional facial features, an innovation inasmuch as the old fashioned rag dolls were made with flat faces.

By contrast, today there are more than 200 different materials that go into the manufacture of a single doll.

Madame Alexander learned at an early age how very important a doll can be to a child. When porcelain dolls were brought in to her father's doll hospital for repair, too often there was a heartbroken child tagging closely behind. And, unfortunately, many of the dolls were beyond repair.

Today, Madame Alexander uses several molding processes to produce sturdy faces, bodies and limbs for her beautiful dolls from the finest durable materials.

Thousands of dolls are bought by collectors each year and passed along from generation to generation within a family.

Madame Alexander dolls are shipped everywhere throughout the world, and her collection of International Dolls featuring the native dress of every UN nation has received recognition at the highest levels. Madame Alexander was honored by U.S. Ambassador to the UN Goldberg at the 1965 United Nations Day (October 22) celebration at New York's City Hall where the full line of International Dolls was on display.

Alice in Wonderland, one of the first Alexander Doll Creations, began a trend that has continued in the firm's selection of doll characters almost from the beginning. Specifically, an Alexander Doll has to contribute to a child's understanding of people, other times and other places.

Hence, Louisa M. Alcott's "Little Women", the Dickens character dolls, Dolls from Storyland, Riley's Little Annie inspired by the Hoosier poet James Whitcomb Riley and "The Sound of Music" dolls.

Madame Alexander inspired by the masterpieces of great painters — Goya, Renoir, Degas, Gainsborough — designed her Portrait children and adult dolls — with all the charm and grace of the era in which they lived, so that children can relate to culture at an early age. Also included in this group, and to introduce to the young of today in celebration of Jenny Lind susquicentennial (1970) — two Jenny Lind dolls. The dolls were inspired by books written about the Swedish Nightingale by Frances Cavanah. "Jenny Lind and her Listening Cat" — portrayed as a nine year old; and "Jenny Lind's America" on her triumphant tour of the United States and Canada. The dolls are a magnificent work of art . . .

Also to be included are the many types of baby dolls created by Madame Alexander such as Baby Genius, Kitten, Huggums, Baby McGuffey, Puddin', Pussy Cat, Victoria, the baby Sweet Tears a great favorite who cries real tears. And the very newest of her baby dolls, "Mary Cassatt Baby" — inspired by one of the paintings of the renowned nineteenth century artist Mary Cassatt.

Always the creative artist in doll designing and manufacture, Madame Alexander does not select a doll for production unless its character has had some personal significance to her. She feels that dolls play an important part in a child's psychological development beginning at about age two. As a child grows, her interest in dolls changes in a steady progression from the baby dolls to older dolls with clothes like the child's own wardrobe.

From the beginning of her career, Madame Alexander has believed strongly that dolls are significant to a child's total educational experience.

Madame Alexander's artistry in doll-making has earned her a life membership in the Brooklyn Institute of Arts and Sciences and her doll collections include one — the collection of Coronation Dolls — which was on exhibition for 11 years at the Brooklyn Children's Museum, New York. In addition, Madame Alexander's dolls are exhibited in many of the museums throughout the world, which include the St. Valentine Museum, Richmond, Va., Museum of Yesteryear, Fla.; The Sandwich Museum, Mass., The Museum of the City of New York.

Upon special request, Madame Alexander designed a grouping of dolls depicting the various cultures of our United States for permanent exhibit at the Congressional Club, Washington, D.C.; and for the Children's Trust Museum, New Delhi, India. These dolls are part of the Americana collection.

In 1968 Madame Alexander was requested to add to their doll collection — and presented to the Smithsonian Institution, Washington, D.C., Madame Doll, portraying the Revolutionary period — and her famous Scarlet O'Hara doll portraying The Civil War era.

In addition to **Madame Alexander, President of the firm,** — considered to be one of the largest independent concerns manufacturing only dolls (an industry which she pioneered shortly after World War I), the family tradition is carried on by **Richard Birnbaum,** her son-in-law who serves as Secretary, and **William Alexander Birnbaum,** her grandson and Vice-President. Philip Behrman, Madame Alexander's late husband, was Vice-President and Treasurer of the company, and **Mildred Birnbaum,** her daughter, offers her artistic services as Research Consultant.

TINA CASTELLI

"LITTLE SHAVER" (1937-1941) One of the first cloth dolls. Inspired from Elsie Saver's paintings of children. Tag: Little Shaver/Madame Alexander.

MUFFIN (1963-1977) The last cloth doll? 14" Felt features, yarn hair. Wears a printed cotton lace- trimmed dress. Flannel diaper. Note: Funny was discontinued also.

COMPOSITION DOLLS

COMPOSITON: A combination of sawdust with a binder (glue, flour, starch, etc). Some companies used more than one binder. In making the first compositon doll, (before the 18th century), the mixture was spread in a cold mold, pressed into shape, and allowed to dry slightly before removing and assembling. With the newer method, the mixture was put into an electric or gas-heated two-piece mold. The doll was moulded and dried in one process. This meant faster production. With the very early composition, parents were very skeptical about purchasing the dolls, due to the rumors of the glue being obtained from slaughter houses. Most glue was made from animal skin, hides, or bones. (Still is!)

Note: All composition dolls are courtesy of the Castelli family, therefore, will not be repeated under each picture.

"Round the World" (1936-1941 Little Betty) Fully jointed composition. Painted eyes, mo-hair wigs. Bodies marked: Mme. Alexander or Wendy Ann. Left to right: Dutch Boy, Dutch Girl, Swiss Girl, Swiss Boy, Swiss Girl, Swiss Boy, Italian, Peasant, Chinese.

This 14″ **PRINCESS ELIZABETH** made her debut the year before her father, King George VI, was crowned the King of England. (1936) On the right: 1937 28″ Both original. Princess Elizabeth was made in 11″-28″.

15″ KATE GREENAWAY 1941
Marked Princess Elizabeth/Madame Alexander on head.

CASTELLI COLLECTION

SONJA HENIE (1910-1969) Dolls came in open/closed mouths. Sizes range from 13"-22". After three Olympic titles in skating, Sonja went into movies with 20th Century Fox.

MARGARET O'BRIEN (1946) 22", 19", 10". Margaret was born in 1937. At seven, she played in the movie, "Meet Me In St. Louis".

FLORA McFLIMSEY, 1939 13″, 15″, 16″. All original. Sleep eyes. All marked: Princess Elizabeth (Doll taken from the McGuffey Reader.)

McGUFFEY ANA 1937-1939 All original composition ranging from 11″-24″.

13" SNOW WHITES 1938 All composition. **Left:** White complexion, tin eyes.

Right: Marked: MMe. Alexander on head. All original.

WENDY ANNS: All composition. Center back row: Painted eyes, molded, painted hair, and swivel waist. Marked: Wendy Ann/MMe. Alexander on head. Front row: All original, open close eyes, mohair wigs.

JEANIE WALKER 18″ is one of only three dolls made in 1943, due to World War II. She is unique because she is made with a wooden piece (she's composition) in the crotch so she can walk. Human hair, sleep eyes. Outfit not original.

13″ "JANE WITHERS" 1937, all original. Marks: Jane Withers/All rights reserved. (As a child, she went from radio into the movies.)

SCARLETT O'HARA This group of Scarletts are all composition, and all original. They range in size from 14″ through 21″. The center doll has original tag.

From the book, "Gone With the Wind," Madame Alexander was inspired to create a Scarlett doll in 1936 and almost every year since. Within a few weeks, over 300,000 books were sold and later, over one million copies.

The movie, released in 1939, was produced by Lewis Selznick. Costumes designed by Walter Plunkett. Trying to find a Scarlett for the role was a difficult job. Lucille Ball, Suzan Hayward, Joan Crawford, Loretta Young, Lana Turner, Betty Davis and Catherine Campbell (Patty Hearst's mother) were a few who tried out for the part. Vivien Hartley, (known to us as Vivien Leigh) became Scarlett O'Hara. Clark Gable played the part of Rhett.

CASTELLI COLLECTION

21" PORTRAITS of 1946. All composition, with hand painted eyelids, eyebrows, and lashes. The Wendy and Margaret molds were used. They retailed for $75.00. The series of 12 dolls include: Carmen, Groom, Judy, King, Queen, Mary Louise, June Bride, Renoir, Camille, Orchard Princess, Princess Rosetta, and Rebecca.

EARLY HARD PLASTIC

MARGARET FACE

These faces were used for approximately 100 different dolls from 1948 through 1955, with the exception of the Maggie face for Little Women in 1956. These dolls were all hard plastic.

FOR A PHOTOGRAPH OF ALL HARD PLASTIC LITTLE WOMEN, SEE SECTION UNDER LITTLE WOMEN.

MAGGIE FACE

COURTESY OF GLENDA CASTELLI

18" BABS (Margaret face) 1949. All hard plastic. Tagged: Babs skating/Madame Alexander. Also made in Maggie face.

18" BABS (Margaret face) 1950. Red jersey blouse with matching panties and stocking cap. Black velveteen jumper, gold skates. Mohair wig. Four leaf clover tag reads: Babs, all rights reserved; Reverse side reads: A Madame Alexander Doll.

11

KAREN BALLERINA 1946 composition. Satin bodice, rayon net skirt. Braided yarn hair. Left: 14" NINA BALLERINA 1950 All hard plastic. Glued on floss wig.

14" CINDERELLA and PRINCE CHARMING (Margaret face) 1950. "They lived happily ever after".

CASTELLI COLLECTION

17″ ALICE-IN-WONDERLAND (Maggie face) 1951. All hard plastic, all original.

MAGGIE 15″, 18″ or 22″ available. 1952-1953. All hard plastic, all original.

CASTELLI COLLECTION

COURTESY OF VELVA GEE

18" ANNABELLE (Maggie face) #1810 1952. This little girl was taken from the book "Stories of Annabelle", and is wearing a pique dress with a "snap down the back" sweater. Available in 15" and 23".

18" CYNTHIA (1952-1953) All hard plastic doll dressed in a luscious pink ruffled dress. 15" and 23".

CASTELLI COLLECTION

VELVA GEE

MADELINE — THE VERY FIRST FULLY JOINTED DOLL OF UNBREAKABLE PLASTIC. Soft molded head, open/close eyes, hair you can wash, and all sorts of clothes and accessories. 18″ only. Marked Alexander on back of head.

MADELINE #1854 1952. She wears an organdy dress with lace trim.

18″ 1952-1953 MADELINE "shows off" in this long sleeved, organdy lace trimmed dress. Her straw hat is partly hidden. She is jointed at the wrists, knees, and elbows.

COURTESY OF META REISTAD

18" #1836 1953 WINSOME WINNIE WALKER wears a swishy taffeta coat with white pique panties and matching dress. She carries a hat box with a comb and curlers. Available in 15" and 25" also. These two dolls are marked Alexander on the head.

25" #2522 1954 WINSOME WINNIE WALKER wears a cotton striped dress with contrasting pinafore. Straw hat, rayon socks, suede shoes. She walks and turns her head from side to side, and is all hard plastic. Same sizes as above doll.

VELVA GEE

GLENDA CASTELLI

21" #2433 1959 SHARI LEWIS, television star, wears a heavy satin skirt, and rayon jersey blouse. Ring, watch, pin, necklace, and earrings.

18″ SWEET VIOLET (Cissy face) 1954. The only fully jointed walking doll ever made. Lavender open/close eyes. Organdy lace trimmed dress, suede shoes. One size only.

8" DOLLS

THIS SECTION IS 8" DOLLS; INCLUDING ALEXANDER-KINS, WENDY-KINS, QUIZ-KINS, INTERNATIONALS, STORYLAND, AND AMERICANA. SEE SEPARATE SECTION FOR LITTLE WOMEN DOLLS.

Alexander-Kins refer to all the little dolls (Quiz-Kins, Little Genius, Maggie Mix-up, and Wendy Ann (Later changed to Wendy).

Wendy-Kins refer to the small dolls, named after Wendy Ann, Madame Alexander's grand-daughter. These include story book and make believe dolls.

The information was taken from the Alexander Doll Company catalogues. The number or numbers (#) following the doll's name are catalogue numbers. Do not rely entirely on these numbers to identify your doll, as stores did not always sell the doll in it's original box. Original means as it came from the factory. Do not be alarmed if you or someone you know has a doll and it's not the exact description or year as shown in this book. Dolls change from year to year, some within the same year.

All dolls are marked ALEX on the back, with the exception of the doll made *after* 1976 and are marked Alexander on the back. The information on the clothing tags may be in red, blue or green. They may read as follows:

Alexander-kins by Madame Alexander, REG U.S. PAT. OFF. N.Y.U.S.A. or, Madame Alexander ALL RIGHTS RESERVED NEW YORK U.S.A. or Alexander-kins "The name" REG. U.S. PAT. OFF. N.Y. U.S.A.

WHEN: 1953

WHO: Alexander-Kins/Wendy Ann*

SIZE: 7½″

HAIR: Glued on wig can be washed, combed, and curled.

FEATURES: Open/close oval eyes, molded upper lashes, painted lower lashes. Dark red mouth.

BODY STRUCTURE: Hard plastic, slightly heavier than any other year. *Straight* leg, jointed at the neck, hips, and shoulders. Slightly tanned body is marked ALEX on the back.

CLOTHING: Approximately 30 outfits were sold separately this year, including: ballerina, bride, Little Southern girl, Peter Pan, Goya, and others.

*Wendy Ann, named after Madame Alexander's grand- daughter.

19

WHEN: 1953-1954

WHO: Quiz-kins

SIZE: 7½″

HAIR: Some came with glued on wigs, some with molded hair.

BODY STRUCTURE: All hard plastic. Nods yes or no, according to the button pushed on the back.

NOTE: Wig on right not original.

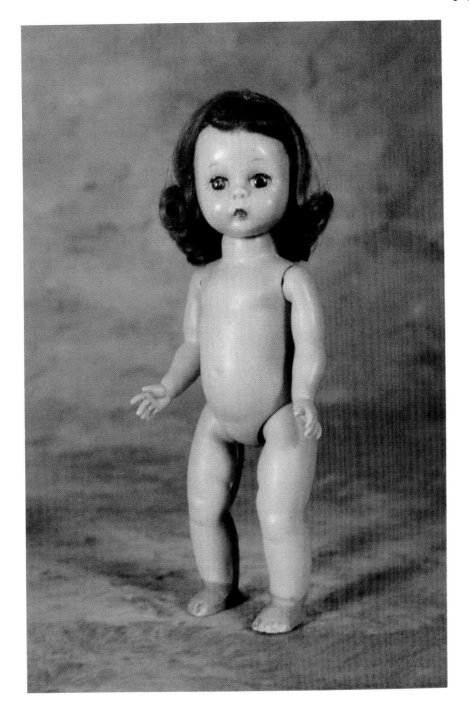

WHEN: 1954-1955

WHO: Alexander-Kins/Wendy*

SIZE: 7½″

HAIR: Glued on washable wig. CAUTION: Do not submerge head, only the hair.

FEATURES: Orange or red mouth. Oval eyes with molded upper lashes, painted lower lashes.

BODY STRUCTURES: Hard plastic, *straight leg walker* (Move her legs back and forth, and she turns her head from side to side.) Light tanned skin and marked ALEX on the back.

CLOTHING: Approximately 45 outfits were made on these dolls. Some of these were: Alice, Queen, Guardian Angel, skaters, and an assortment of outfits were available in separate packages.

OTHER INFORMATION: In *1954* Old Testament Bible Characters were available. Bill, named after Madame Alexander's grandson, was made. Four dolls were copies of the 18″ dolls. They are Elaine, Queen, Louise, and Victoria.
In *1955* Little Women were offered, along with Hansel, Gretel, Red Riding Hood, Bo Peep, and Scarlett. Many other outfits and accessories were available. Too, in 1955, *Ann was dropped from the name Wendy Ann, due to her death.

WHEN: 1956-1965

WHO: Alexander-Kins/Wendy

SIZE: 7½″

HAIR: Glued on washable wig. CAUTION: Submerge hair only, not the head.

FEATURES: Red lips, oval eyes, molded upper lashes and painted lower lashes.

BODY STRUCTURE: Hard plastic, *jointed knee walkers.* Jointed also at the neck, shoulders and hips. Pink bodies marked ALEX on back.

CLOTHING: *(1956)* Approximately 75 outfits were made.

OTHER INFORMATION:
1960.   Maggie Mix-Up and Little Lady dolls were made with the rosebud or watermellon (smiling) mouths.
1961.   The Internationals were started; making Dutch Girl, French, Italian, Spanish Girl, Swiss, Swedish, and Scots Las. The Americana group (derived from the cultures of the U.S.) was started with four old-fashioned girl   outfits.
1962.   Hungarian, Tyrolean Boy and Girl were added to the internationals. Some of these had a watermellon   mouth (smiling). Scots Las was changed to Scottish. American Girl and Colonial Girl were added to the   Americana series.
1963.   The outfits were tagged Wendy-kins instead of Alexander-kins.
1965.   The last year the Wendy-kin label was used. Started discontinuing walkers.

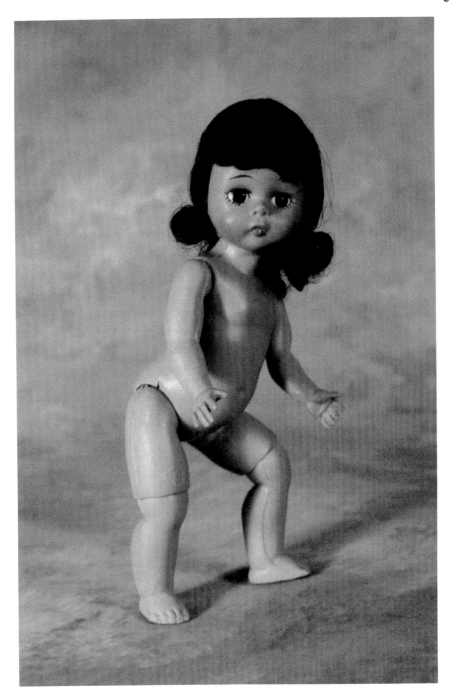

WHEN: 1966-1972

WHO: Internationals, Storyland, Americana and Little Women.

SIZE: 7½″

HAIR: Glued on wig.

FEATURES: Red-orange mouths (some are darker). Painted lower lashes, molded uppers. Cheek color varies.

BODY STRUCTURE: Hard plastic, *jointed knees.* Tanned or pink bodies.

OTHER INFORMATION:
1968. A limited edition of "Easter Doll" was available. This doll was designed by our West Coast Representative for the Madame Alexander Company.
1972. Snow White and Alice were made exclusively for Disneyland/World.

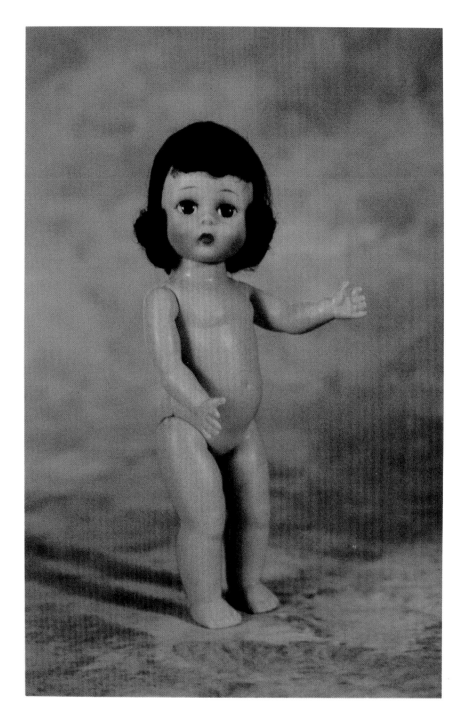

WHO: Internationals, Storyland, Little Women

WHEN: 1973-1976

SIZE: 7½″

HAIR: Glued on wig.

FEATURES: Painted lower lashes, molded upper.

BODY STRUCTURE: Hard plastic, *straight legs*. Powdery, pink body. Marked ALEX on back.

WHO: Internationals, Storyland, and Little Women.

WHEN: 1977 to date.

SIZE: 7½″

HAIR: Glued on wig.

FEATURES: Mouth more puckered looking, except on the tanned Oriental dolls, which have a full, rounded face. Molded upper lashes. The painted lower lashes are slightly higher past the corners of the eyes than on any other doll.

BODY STRUCTURE: *Straight legs* with joints only at the neck, shoulders, and hips. Powdery pink or tanned Oriental body marked ALEXANDER on the back.

NOTE: All small dolls are marked ALEX on the back before 1977.

#453 1955 This **ALEXANDER-KIN** walks in the rain, wearing a pink matching coat and hat.

COURTESY OF IVA LANCE

ALEXANDER-KIN plays in her white pique sunsuit trimmed in red. Notice her red suede shoes.

#383 1960 WENDY BRIDE wears a pink bridal dress of nylon tulle with a satin sash. Her veil is attached to a coronet of flowers to match her bouquet. She is a jointed knee walker.

Dressed alike, WENDY and brother BILL, wear cotton knit sweaters with brass buttons. Her pleated skirt and his short pants are attached to a white pique top. Both are jointed knee walkers. Her tag reads: "Wendy Kin" by Madame Alexander New York, U.S.A. His reads; Madame Alexander All rights reserved New York U.S.A.

KAY GAUGHAN

SCARLETT #631 1956 This little lady is dressed in a beautiful flowered gown. She wears a floral decorated straw hat, and carries a parasol.

TERI FROEHLICH

An assortment of **ALEXANDER-KIN/WENDY-KIN** clothes, which could have been purchased separately. Many others were available.

AMISH BOY #726 (1966-1969) A follower of Jacob Amman, a Mennonite (a Protestant Christian sect founded in the 16th Century). He introduced the religious observance of feet-washing and the avoidance of every kind of luxury, even the wearing of buttons on clothing. These observances are still followed today in Europe and the U.S.

ALICE IN WONDERLAND (1972-1976) Cotton dress with white collar, white braid trim. White socks, panties, petticoat. Were available only at Disneyland/World. Tagged: "Alice" Walt Disney Prod. 1975 by Madame Alexander.

ARGENTINA GIRLS #771, 571 (1965 to date) These dolls have brown eyes, dark brown braids. Petite flowers scattered on a one piece V-neck dress with bottom ruffle. White cotton lace, trimmed slip, pantalettes. Three dolls to show a variety of prints.

Listed clockwise: First two dolls were made from 1973-1976. Very front doll is 1977, the new faced doll marked ALEXANDER on the back.

AUSTRIA GIRL #598 (1974 to date) (Was TYROLEAN from 1962-1973) This cutie has a red flowered skirt with green velveteen top. Organdy sleeves are lace trimmed. Her blonde braided hair is tied with two ribbons. She wears long red socks, black shoes and green hat.

NOTE: Skirt came in various prints. Hat in brown, or green.

AUSTRIA BOY #599 (1974 to date) (Was TYROLEAN from 1962-1973) This little guy has a white organdy shirt under flowered suspenders that support his velveteen pants. He stays warm under a green felt jacket. His brown hat can't conceal his rich blonde hair and blue eyes.

NOTE: Earlier dolls had beige shoes.

NOTE: SEE TYROLEAN

BALLERINA (1953 to date) While these BALLERINAS dance, let me tell you a little about them. Their ballet dresses (tou tous) came in white, yellow, pink or blue, but not every color every year. Their eyes were brown or blue and their hair was blonde, brunette, auburn, or tosca (brownish blonde). One in pink is 1976, one in blue is 1972.

BELGIUM #762,562 (1972 to date) This brown eyed little lady wears a peppermint striped apron over a long sleeved dress. Under her white hat is long brown hair. Her half cotton slip covers her pantalettes.

BETSY ROSS #431 (1976 to date) According to legend, the maker of the first American flag. In observance of the bi-centennial year.

BETSY ROSS #731, 431 (1967 to date) They wear blue printed cotton dresses. Mob caps, sleeves, and shawls are trimmed with cotton eyelet. Undies and aprons are white. Tosca hair is pulled into a bun. They have blue eyes. Both have jointed knees.

COURTESY OF META REISTAD

BO PEEP #383,783,483 (1962 to date)
Little Bo-Peep has lost her sheep, And can't tell where to find them; Leave them alone, and they'll come home, Wagging their tails behind them.

BRAZIL #773,573 (1965 to date) "Too beautiful for words".

NOTE: Some of the earlier dolls were made with earrings, and four strands of beads. Before 1971, they wore straw hats.

GEORGEANN TINTORI

AMERICANA BRIDE #735 "Here comes the BRIDE" in a lovely lace-edged gown with matching veil. Beneath her tulle gown is white taffeta laced panties, full slip and blue elastic garter. Who'll catch her flower bouquet?

VELVA GEE

BRIDE #735 (1966-1970) GROOM (1956) Bride same as above, groom wears a white suedine shirt with tie, and gray cumberbund. Pinstripe pants and "stiff" tuxedo.

NOTE: These two dolls were shown from 1953-1963.

BRIDES #435 (Current blonde) #735 (Jointed knee brunette)
"Blondes have more fun."
This brunette doesn't agree.

NOTE: Lace edging differs from previous dolls.

CANADA #760,560 (1968 to date) This lovely doll
shows brown curls from under a white poke bonnet.
Under an off-white flowered dress, she wears white taffeta can can and pantaloons edged in lace.

NOTE: Dress prints vary, as do the collars. Undies
came in cotton on most dolls.

CHINA #772,572 (1972 to date) "Chinadoll" is a full 7½″ tall. Her brown hair and "cooley" hat accentuate her flirty black eyes. Her aqua brocade coat shines as she walks. Through her black trousers can be seen a slight wiggle. Rice paddies would flourish in the presence of this doll.

CZECHOSLAVAKIA #764,564 (1972 to date) She has brown eyes and her center part wig is pulled back into curls. A circular felt skirt is attached to a velveteen bodice. To top it all off is a red and green hat.

DENMARK #769,569 (1970 to date)
My eyes are blue, my tag is too.
My dress of maroon sheen, accents
my bonnet and apron of green.
My pantalettes and socks of white
set off my shoes, the color of night.
Now that you've found me in this
book, take a very long long look.

DUTCH BOY #777,577 (1964-1973) Changed to
Netherlands in 1974. Dutch Boy stops to wave.
He wears a red felt jacket and blue velveteen
pants. His hat is black, shoes tan. These shoes
were later replaced with wooden shoes.

DUTCH GIRL #391,491,791,591 (1961-1973)
Changed to Netherlands in 1974. As she walks,
(she's a walker) her wood shoes click against the
cobblestones. A gentle breeze lifts her blue tafetta dress and reveals her red socks and white pantalettes. She holds her little flower basket against
her white apron, and sighs, "Oh what a day."

TERI FROEHLICH

8" EASTER DOLL (1968) Lace trimmed dress with matching bonnet. Nylon tights, white side snap shoes. Made in 14" also. Only 300 were made; at the request of our West Coast Sales Representative for the Alexander Company.

(NOTE: Suppose he could put in another request?)

ECUADOR #387,787 (1963-1966) A South American country astride the equator (from which it derives its name). In the plateau basins, where the temperatures average 55°, Ecuador wears an orange, trimmed skirt and an overskirt of olive green. Both skirts are attached to a white blouse edged in crocheted trim. She's off to catch the train, on one of the most picturesque railroads in the world.

VELVA GEE

39

YVONNE GADBERRY

ENGLISH GUARD #764 (1966-1968) This Palace guard stands at attention. He wears a furry black hat and cotton pants (side stripe). He is complete with a red felt jacket.

ESKIMO #723 (1966-1969) This Eskimo boy isn't as cold as he looks. He keeps warm in his "fur" cuffed pants and suede boots. His black eyes peer out from under his felt parka as he searches for his pet seal.

NOTE: Pants came with or without "fur" trim. Parka braid came in green also.

YVONNE GADBERRY

FINLAND #761,561 (1968 to date) Fashioned well; decorated black dress, red hat, white knee-high socks, bodice, pantaloons, and black shoes. Her eyes resemble the sky and her hair the morning sun.

FRANCE #390,490,790,590 (1961 to date) French are noted for their love and style of fashions. This fine Miss wears white lacy hat, slip, and pantaloons. While in Paris, she chose this navy blue and white striped dress with lemon yellow overskirt pulled up in a swag effect and accented with a bow. Eyes and hair are brown.

NOTE: Earlier dolls carried a basket and wore black and white striped skirt.

GERMANY #763,563 (1966 to date) Hi! I'm Germany. My flowered dress and apron were made for this occasion. I'm careful not to muss my long blonde curls and velveteen hat. My dress covers my long white stockings and pantalettes.

GREAT BRITIAN #558 (1977 to date) This new member of the Alexander family wears a black bodice attached to a black/white striped skirt. Long sleeves are half black, half white. She wraps a brightly colored fichu* around her shoulders. A white bonnet and black hat match her outfit perfectly.

*A three-cornered cape with the ends crossed or tied in the front.

GREECE #765,565 (1968 to date) This elegant girl displays a yellow apron over a black skirt. Her dark brown hair is covered with an elasticized shawl, accented with flowers.

GREEK BOY #769 (1965-1968) This Greek Royal Guard parades in full-dress uniform.

GRETEL and HANSEL #754,454 (1966 to date) and #753,453 (1966 to date) Lost in the woods, Hansel comforts Gretel. He wears red hat and pants, flowered shirt. He has blue eyes, blonde hair. Gretel wears a flowered bonnet and apron to accent a red skirt. She has blue eyes, platinum hair.

HAWAIIAN #722 (1966-1969) I'm a suntan beauty with brown eyes and hair. Around my neck a lei of green net, trimmed with flowers. My bikini top is embroidered flowers on green elastic. My grass skirt, attached to pink undies, is just right for dancing. Come hula with me.

HUNGARY #397,597 (1962 to date) Like Christmas, Hungary turns into a spectrum of color: gold jeweled crown, felt laced vest, zig zag trimmed dress, red suede boots, and a red bow on each blonde pigtail. "She is a doll!"

NOTE: The metal crown has been discontinued and replaced with a rhinestone and braid trimmed tiara.

INDIA #775,575 (1965 to date) Beneath their white veils, they wear dark brown hair pulled into a center back braid. Their aqua- blue dresses are trimmed in gold. Half tricot slips are attached to the dress. Jewelry consists of gold chain necklace, snake charm bracelet, and (maybe) earrings. Gold sandals.

NOTE: Two different skin colors. Older dolls had coin earrinngs.

INDIAN BOY #720 (1966); HIAWATHA #720, (1967-1969) "Heep big hunter" wears a tan suede vest and woven clouts sewn to brown "buckskin" breeches.

CASTELLI COLLECTION

INDONESIA #779,579 (1970 to date) Indonesia has tan skin, black pupilless eyes and brown hair. She stands barefoot in a red and black brocade skirt. Part of her long sleeved black bodice is hidden behind her black panel. She is superb with her gold sash, collar, and cone hat.

IRELAND #778,578 (1964 to date) An Irish redhead. Her green taffeta dress and flowered shawl compliment her green eyes. Her bonnet, apron, pantaloons and petticoat are all edged in crocheted lace.

NOTE: Most dresses came in cotton. Prints and edgings vary.

ISREAL #768,568 (1965 to date) Isreal, "sitting pretty" with eyes of blue and brown pigtails laying on her tiny white blouse. She wears a taffeta skirt, tan sandals and trimmed slip and panties.

JOEY BIGGS

ITALY #393,493,793,593 (1961 to date) Representing the boot shaped country, Italy wears a braid trimmed dress to accent a green apron. Beneath her folded down hat, she displays brown hair, and eyes, and tiny earrings.

NOTE: Earrings discontinued.

JAPAN #770,570 (1968 to date) Petite Japanese lady, tanned skin, black eyes, and brown hair. Aqua brocade kimona - red pants, paper umbrella in hand. She stands with dignity at the Tanababate Festival in Tokyo.

KOREA #772 (1968-1970) This doll wears a gold and purple robe. Her one piece red and white tafetta dress covers her white panties and hip high stockings. She has black suede shoes and a gold and green headpiece. As you pass, she smiles.

1960 MAGGIE MIX-UP is an adorable doll with a pixie face, a freckled nose, and long straight red hair. She loves to wear this perky blue dress with veiled hat. Green eyes, watermellon mouth.

MARY MARY #751,451 (1965 to date) This group of Mary Mary's was chosen to show a variety of dress prints. However, aprons, hair and eye color are all the same.

Back row, left to right: 1967 jointed knee, 1973 straight leg, 1978 new puckered face, and sitting, 1975.

MEXICO #776,576 (1964 to date) This Mexican senorita has brown eyes and long brown braid . Her hat is trimmed with green and red braid. Beneath her black skirt she wears laced pantalettes and petticoat. Knee-high socks, black shoes with tiny gold buttons. "Mucho lindo"

MISS MUFFET #752,452 (1965 to date) Miss Muffet, decked in blue dress and pink mob cap, was surprised upon seeing the spider, which dangled beside her.

MOROCCO #762 (1968-1970) (An Arab Kingdom in Northwest Africa) With sandals and dress of gold, this black- eyed brown-haired lady stands, skin tinted by the sun. She wears matching headband and cumberbund. Her rainbow robe touches the sand as she looks over the city of Fez.

NETHERLANDS BOY #577 (1974 to date), NETHERLANDS GIRL #591 (1974 to date) Called Dutch before 1974."Wooden Shoe" picture us in the land of tulips and windmills?

NOTE: For description, see Dutch.

NORWAY #784,584 (1968 to date) Miss Norway, a blue eyed brunette, wears white cotton pantalettes under her black dress. She also wears a lovely long sleeved white top and a puffy white hat.

PERUVIAN BOY #770 (1965-1966) A descendant of the South American Inca Indians, this boy has blue eyes, brown hair, green hat, tweed pants and tan sandals. He wears a bright colored woven poncho while playing a gay tune.

NOTE: Guitar has been added.

SHANE BIGGS

53

POLAND #780,580 (1964 to date)
Sitting amongst the leaves and rocks,
she is careful not to dirty her white
dress.

PORTUGAL #785,585 (1968 to date) She is a
million dollar baby. Along with black hat, gold
scarf, green shawl, pink skirt and pantaloons,
she's worth every dollar.

PRISCILLA #789 (1965) #729 (1966-1970); FORMERLY COLONIAL GIRL #389 (1962-1963) #789 (1964) Priscilla was taken from Henry Wadsworth Longfellow's poem, "Courtship of Miles Standish." The Puritan maiden Priscilla Mullens was courted by John Alden, as proxy for Miles Standish. The poem was based on traditional and historical accounts of an incident in early New England.

REDBOY #740,440 (1972 to date) In the 1800's Red Boy, the Prime Minister of Spain, was Queen Luisa's secret lover. But not secret to Francisco de Goya, who painted him. Goya was known for his portraits and etchings of Spanish royalty.

RED RIDING HOOD #382,782,482 (1962 to date) Little Red Riding Hood making her way to Grandma's house with her basket of flowers.

ROMANIA/RUMANIA #786,586 (1968 to date) She wears a full baby blue dress bordered with tiny flowers. Her black apron, trimmed with red roses, sets off her black shoes and bucket hat. She wears white trimmed pantaloons and slip over white knee-high socks. Her brown hair is braided into a single strand.

RUSSIA #774,574 (1965 to date) Blue-eyed, brown haired Russia models a red skirt, crochet trimmed blouse. Full can can, white pantalettes and suede boots.

NOTE: Earlier dolls had braided hair, current dolls have hair twisted across the head and tied at one side.

SCARLETT O'HARA #725 (1966-1972) Any collector would cherish this Scarlett wearing a cotton rosebud dress and picture hat of straw.

SCARLETT #725,425 (1973 to date) Scarlett in a dainty organdy dress, tied around the waist with a green sash. "Hidden" is a full petticoat and cotton pantaloons, both trimmed in lace.

SCOTLAND #396,496,796,596 (1961 to date) Scotland has green eyes and brown hair. Her pleated skirt (kilt), scarf, and tam, are red plaid and attached to a sleeveless bodice with center lace trim. She carries a small purse (sporran). Jacket and socks are green. White panties.

TONY BIGGS

DWARFS COURTESY OF META REISTAD

SNOW WHITE (1972-1976) White taffeta panties, lace trimmed. Crinoline half slip. Pantihose. Made for Disneyland/World only. Tagged: "Snow White" Walt Disney Prod. 1975 By Madame Alexander.

SPANISH GIRL #395,495,795,595 (1961 to date); SPANISH BOY #779 (1964-1968) The band plays, and senora twirls. Her red dress, with flounces, trimmed in black lace floats out. A mantilla covers her brown hair. The senor's red tie and cumberbund make his outfit complete.

SWEDEN #392,492,792,592 (1961 to date) In a red cotton dress, she steps out for a stroll. She wears a green taffeta apron lined with flowers. A black flowered bonnet and shawl help to offset the charm of her blue eyes and blonde hair. Frilly petticoat and pantaloons. How heavenly!

SWISS #394,494,794,594 (1961 to date) Switzerland is dressed in an organdy braid trimmed blouse sewn to a red felt skirt. She has on a green alpine cap and wears red ribbons on her golden braids. Her apron is white lace.

COURTESY OF TINA FERGUSON

THAILAND #767,567 (1966 to date) "Having a ball", are these black eyed, brown haired cuties. Their gold sandals, hats, and trim dominate their attire. Aqua blue pants, and metalic colored blouses are a striking combination. Center doll is 1968, left is 1977 (New), right is 1976.

NOTE: Some dolls were made with brown eyes.

TURKEY #787,587 (1968 to date) Turkey's eyes and hair are brown. Under her flowered metalic jacket is hidden a yellow cumberbund. Her bloomer pants puff out over her gold shoes. To top it all off, she wears a red hat.

TYROLEAN BOY #399,499,799,599;
TYROLEAN GIRL #398,498,798,598
(1962-1973 made as Tyrolean.) 1974
to date made as Austria. For description, see Austria.

"UNITED STATES" #599 (1974 to date) This
pretty miss wears a dress of taffeta. Her white
organdy shawl, mob hat, half slip and pantalettes are trimmed with white lace. She has blonde
hair worn with a center part and pulled into two
barrel curls and tied. "She's sure to be a winner."

NOTE: Some dolls were labeled "Untied States".

VIETNAM #788 (1968-1969) She smiles and her picture is taken. She is wearing a sleeveless white top joined to black pants. Pink brocade top is lined in blue, and split up both sides. Underneath her coolie hat is a brown bun.

YUGOSLAVIA #789,589 (1968 to date) Yugoslavia could charm anyone in this polka-dotted skirt. Below her ribbon and lace trimmed bodice is a ric-rac and braid trimmed apron. Covering her tosca bun are two headscarves. She shows white can can and black boots.

NOTE: Some dolls had their hair pulled back into small curls; this one wears a bun.

MADAME ALEXANDER MAKES A
COMPLETE LINE OF BABY DOLLS.
THIS SECTION CONTAINS SOME OF
THE DISCONTINUED ONES.

LITTLE GENIUS (Wendy's baby sister) (1956-1962) An adorable 8" jointed vinyl baby with a hard plastic head. She drinks and wets, and even goes to sleep with her bottle. Doll is unmarked. She has a saran wig. Her clothes are tagged "Little Genius" Madame Alexander Reg. U.S. Pat. Off. N.Y.U.S.A.

#756 1957 LITTLE GENIUS has on an embroidered organdy dress with matching bonnet.

1956 "BABY GENIUS" in a satin lined bunting.

COURTESY OF KAY GAUGHAN.

#242 1957 BABY GENIUS wears a soft printed cotton dress with a tucked yoke.

BABY GENIUS Lace, feather stitching, and two tiny buttons decorate this darling dress. Soft yellow slip, socks, and bonnet go with her white side snap shoes.

"LITTLE GENIUS" is ready for bed, in this long flannel gown, with matching diaper panties.

COURTESY OF CASTELLI COLLECTION

LITTLEST KITTEN (1963-1964) 8″ all soft vinyl baby with moving eyes and lashes. Could be purchased dressed, or as a basic doll in undies, then you could complete the wardrobe of your choice.

LITTLEST KITTEN on the left: A 5c garage sale special. On the right. One outfit from a large variety of clothes.

SWEET TEARS "9″ (1965-1973) This soft vinyl baby is fully jointed. She came in sprayed and rooted hair. She drinks, wets, and cries real tears. The following are some of the outfits she came in; pin-dotted cotton dress, pink organdy dress, Christening dress, bunting, pin checked ruffled cotton dress, gingham dress, pink tricot robe, and various layettes.

NOTE: Organdy lace trimmed dress, flannel diaper, booties, available in 14″ or 16″ dolls.

META REISTAD

#3266 14″ BABY McGUFFEY has on a pink cotton dress with puffed sleeves. Over her dress is a darling white eyelet pinafore and matching bonnet. White socks, kid pumps are added. 20″ doll was discontinued in 1977.

#5360 (1969-1970) MARY CASSATT BABY was inspired by the 19th century artist, Mary Cassatt. She wears a cotton lace trimmed dress under a white pinafore trimmed with blue feather stitching. White socks, pink kid pumps. An adorable blue straw hat with flower trim.

COURTESY OF VELVA GEE

"LITTLE WOMEN" were inspired from the book written by Louisa Mae Alcott (1832-1888). The book reveals the daily home life, adventures, and love affairs of Meg, Amy, Jo, and Beth. The family life and minor crises of the small New England community are evidently derived from the author's own girlhood.

In 1949 the movie "Little Women" was released starring Elizabeth Taylor as Amy, Margaret O'Brien as Beth, Janet Leigh as Meg, Mary Astor as Marme, June Allyson as Jo, and Peter Lawford as Laurie.

The trademark for "Little Women" was taken out in 1933, and there has been a set available almost every year since.

The following 8" dolls have short, white socks and black side snap shoes, unless noted. All are jointed knee walkers made from 1956-1965.

BETH 1960 Brown hair tied at the top with pink bow. Pink dress has two rows of trim. Undies have embroidered edging.

70

JO 1958 Blue eyed brunette. Floor length red jumper over a longsleeve organdy blouse. Embroidered trim on lower edge of petticoat and pantaloons. Red side snap shoes, white socks.

JO 1960 Tiny black dots on a white cotton dress, red pinafore accented with white rick rack. Full can can and pantaloons.

JO 1963 She wears a blue and white printed jumper, attached to a long sleeved organdy blouse. Half red apron.

META REISTAD COLLECTION

AMY 1960 This blue eyed blonde wears a long sleeved dress and a tiny flowered apron. Lace trimmed can can and pantaloons.

AMY 1963 White organdy pinafore over polkadot dress; both lace trimmed.

MEG 1957 Tosca hair, blue eyes. Lavender dress with organdy collar. Striped pinafore has three rows of zig zag trim. Cotton half slip and pantaloons.

1955 MEG'S tiny blue apron matches her flowered dress with organdy collar and trimmed sleeves.

TERI FROEHLICH

73

MARME 1958 Red plaid dress, black apron, organdy fischu and brooch. Pantaloons and slip are complete with crocheted edging.

MARME (Mother) 1960 Blue eyes, brunette hair pulled into a bun. She wears a green tafetta dress accented with black braided trim. Her ice green apron is bordered in black lace. An organdy shawl covers her shoulders and shows a brooch. Undies trimmed in crocheted stitch.

LISSY was used for Little Women from 1956-1967. Some were made using the jointed Lissy doll, and others with the Lissy face and the 12" Elise body. (Pinkie, Blueboy, etc.)

MEG (Lissy face), wears a striped cotton dress and cotton undies. This doll has the Lissy face with the 12" Elise body.

NOTE: See AMY under the LISSY section.

LISSY BETH-jointed Lissy body. Pink/white checked dress. Apron, pantaloons and slip all trimmed in crocheted edging. Green eyes, brown hair. Black strap sandals, white socks.

8″ LITTLE WOMEN-LAURIE (1966-1972) Jointed knee

	LAURIE	
MEG		MARME
BETH		JO
	AMY	

ALL these and the following 8″ Little Women have cotton half slips, pantaloons, white socks and black side snap shoes, blue or brown eyes. MARME (Mother) wears a maroon full-skirted dress. Embroidery trimmed apron and lace trimmed duster cap.

The following are 8″ Little Women made from 1973-1976, except Beth, which is a 1977 to date doll. All are straight leg.

AMY Cotton dress with polka dot pinafore. Blonde curls atop her head are accented with a bow.

8″ LAURIE (1969 to date) courted Jo, and married Amy. Wearing navy blue jackets, striped or checked pants.

BETH Baby (she's the baby of the family). Pink dress with organdy lace trimmed pinafore. Matching pink bow holds her top curls in place.

MEG Checked, long sleeved dress. Pinafore with four rows of chain stitching and row of crocheted edging. Tosca hair tied on top with a tiny bow.

JO Red cotton dress with eyelet apron, full petticoat, and pantaloons.

12" LITTLE WOMEN — LAURIE This body structure was used for these dolls in 1968 to date. Laurie was added in 1970 and is currently made. The clothing descriptions are the same as the 8" dolls.

15" LITTLE WOMEN (1948-1956) All hard plastic, all original. They have rayon socks, black side snap shoes with a tiny bow on the front of each toe. All have cotton petticoats attached to their dresses and fancy trimmed cotton pantaloons. Individually styled hair fashions. The dress tags read: Louisa M. Alcott's Little Women "The name" by Madame Alexander, N.Y. U.S.A. All rights reserved. Marked ALEX on back of head. Original price tags read: $7.95. Some sets had large open fingers, while this set has small closed-finger hands. Complexion colors came in light or dark. Pictured clockwise; Marme (Margaret face), Beth (Maggie face), Meg and Amy (Margaret face), and Jo (Maggie face).

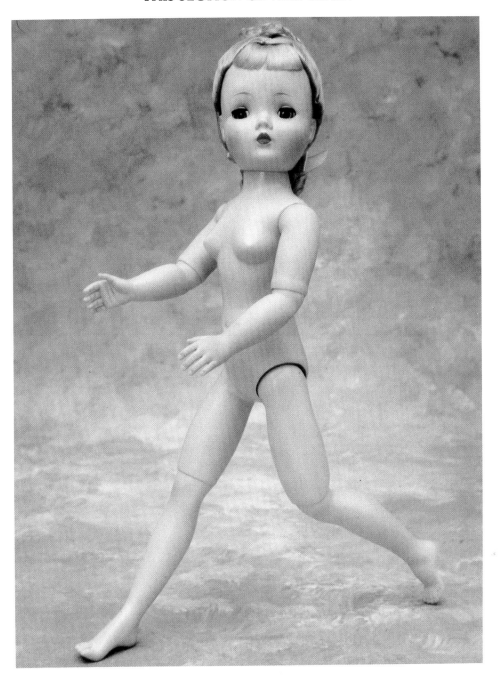

CISSY (1955-1959)* As Cissy "streaks" by, glimpse her tall slim plastic body, molded bosom, jointed elbows and knees. Observe her high-heeled feet. She made her first public appearance (debut) in *1955,* although her face was used in *1953* and *1954* on such dolls as Binnie and Winnie Walker, Sweet Violet, Active Miss, and others. Cissy came fully clothed or as a basic doll. (Just undies). *1955* Cissy was pictured in the catalogue as seven Portraits and in three other outfits. A large line of apparel and accessories could be purchased separately. *1956-1957* Cissy was offered in a variety of outfits, in addition to eight various formals. *1958,* once again, six Portrait dolls and a sideline of fashions were available. *1959* only three outfits were shown in the catalogue, along with a few items sold separately.

*1961 Cissy face was used as Portrait Queen, Melanie, and Scarlett O'Hara.

*1962 Offered as Queen Elizabeth II of England. Extra clothes available.

VELVA GEE

Basic CISSY #2100. Nylon lace chemise*, long nylon hose, and mules** trimmed with flowers and lace. Her shinny hair can be washed, curled, and combed. Her shadow is basic "CISSETTE" #900.

*chemise - a loose under garment resembling a short slip. **mules - a backless lounging slipper.

CISSY models a low cut rosebud negligee with matching robe. Both are trimmed in lace and blue bows. Very sexy!

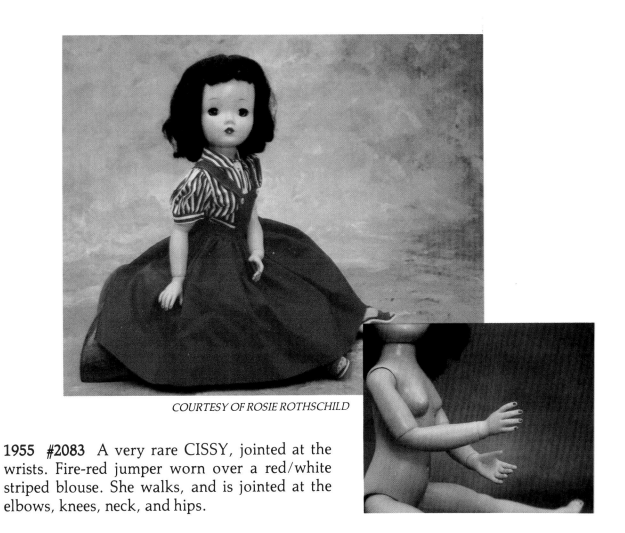

COURTESY OF ROSIE ROTHSCHILD

1955 #2083 A very rare CISSY, jointed at the wrists. Fire-red jumper worn over a red/white striped blouse. She walks, and is jointed at the elbows, knees, neck, and hips.

CISSY #2140 1957 Madame Alexander chose this navy taffeta dress with crisp layered cape for Cissy to wear. Accessories include straw hat with flowers, pearl drop earrings, bracelet, and French gloves.

#2120 1957 CISSY goes shopping in this lovely flowered dress, straw hat, white gloves and shoes.

COURTESY OF GEORGEANN TINTORI.

#2118 21″ CISSY loves to wear this beautiful lavender dress with a white linen coat. Under these, she has on nylon hose, flocked, scalloped petticoat, and white taffeta panties. Atop her shinny blond hair "sits" a fur hat decorated with violets and green leaves. Matching lavender shoes, and rhinestone earrings.

#2281 1958 CISSY QUEEN walks in dignity while wearing a fully lined brocade gown with train effect; hooped crinoline slip, yellow panties, nylons and gold sling backs. Her jewelry consists of tear drop earrings, 3 rhinestone bracelets and a ring.

#2285 1958 For a very special occasion, CISSY wears this hollyberry gown with polka-dotted stole. She wears a ring, pearl drop earrings, and pearl necklace.

#2282 1958 CISSY PORTRAIT At a garden party, Cissy strolls in a three-skirted gown of tulle, organdy, and taffeta. Her large sheer hat is trimmed with white roses. Her accessories include gloves, pearl necklace and bracelet.

THIS SECTION COVERS CISSETTE, INCLUDING: JACQUELINE, PORTRETTES, AND DOLLS MADE FROM THE CISSETTE MOLD. (10½")

CISSETTE

The name "Cissette" refers to the 11″ mold produced by Madame Alexander in 1957 and used through 1973. The doll is 10½″ tall, life-like in color, has jointed knees and high-heeled feet. In the catalogue, Madame Alexander describes "Cissette" by saying, "she looks like a real person, tiny and perfect." And that she does! "Cissettes" were sold fully dressed, or as a basic doll in a chemise* and mules**, or in a pink crepe slip and taffeta panties. If a basic doll was bought, you could then select and purchase the clothes of your choice.

1960 The "Cissette" face was used for the flat footed, unjointed, "Sleeping Beauty", made only for Disneyland.

1961 Margo made her debut. Using the "Cissette" mold, Margo had a new hairdo, blue eye shadow, and heavier eyeliner.

1962 Jacqueline was made with a wardrobe designed with "the best of taste", including a formal, two piece suit, evening gown, and sports outfit. "Cissette" was made in a few international costumes, but the 8″ dolls were much more popular.

1963 A bubble hair cut was in. Some dolls also had removable and interchangable wigs.

1968 Due to special demand, a miniature Portrait doll was issued. (Called Portrette). There were six Portrettes made each year through 1970. 1968 dolls: #1170 - Southern Belle, #1171 - Agatha, #1172 - Godey, #1173 - Melinda, #1174 - Scarlett, #1175 - Renoir.

1969 The same as 1968, with the exception of #1171 which was changed to Jenny Lind. Tinkerbelle, the Magic Fairy from the motion picture "Peter Pan" was made.

1970 The same names were available with Melanie replacing Melinda. The numbers were 80's instead of 70's. (#1182, 1183, etc.). Too, the Small Sound of Music Brigetta, Liesl, and Louisa were made through 1973.

1971 #1181 Scarlett and #1185 Southern Belle were added.

1972 Added #1186 the Queen.

1973 Same three dolls were made with different numbers. (#1187 Queen, #1184 Southern Belle, and #1180 Scarlett.)

*A loose undergarment resembling a short slip.
**A backless lounging slipper.

Guides in dating "Cissettes"

CLOTHING TAGS: All tags are printed in turquoise except 1963, which is blue.

DRESS DARTS: 1957-1959 bodice darts were used.
　　　　　　　　1960-1963 no darts, with the exception of formal wear.

WIGS: 1957-1958 three rows of stitching
　　　　1959-1963 zig zag stitching

FINGERNAILS: 1957-1960 no polish
　　　　　　　　1960-1963 polish (Note: Some with and without polish in 1960)

EYE LIDS: 1957 beige
　　　　　　1958 pale pink, all other years pink.

EYE WEIGHTS: 1957-1958 heavy eye weights.
　　　　　　　　1958-1963 light eye weights. (Heavy and light weights in 1958)

1957 #900 Lace chemise*, nylon hose, and mules.** Some had earrings.

*A loose undergarment resembling a short slip.
**A backless lounging slipper.

1958 #801 Basic Cissette wears lace trimmed crepe slip with tiny flowers. Taffeta panties hidden beneath.

"CISSETTE" Left: 1958 #807 Blue velvet pants with a lace blouse and sash of starched chiffon. Pearl necklace and earrings. Right: #905 1957 Black velvet toreador pants with sheer lace blouse fastened with rhinestones. Taffeta sash accents her tiny waistline.

1957 #0931 CISSETTE wearing a reversible coat and hat for rain or shine.

Cissette #808 1958 While yachting, Cissette relaxes in white pants and a nautical jacket with brass buttons. Sun glasses protect her eyes.

1958 - #810 Cotton dress with braid trim. White straw hat.

CISSETTE BALLERINA'S wear ballet outfits with layers and layers of nylon tulle attached to a satin body suit. Flowers adorn their hair and tou tous. Each was in a box marked Cissette #823, but not listed in the catalogues.

VELVA GEE

CISSETTE #735 1962 Four layers of nylon tulle, pink tights, and dainty ballet slippers make this one beautiful ballerina. Rhinestone earrings, and a coronet of flowers in her hair.

VELVA GEE

1957 #971 Queen Elizabeth II in a gold brocade gown, worn with the blue Sash of the Garter. Elegantly styled jeweled tiara, rhinestone earrings, bracelet, and pearl necklace.

1962 #760 "GIBSON GIRL" is wearing a purple velveteen skirt, striped lavender blouse, feathers on her hat. Note: In 1963 the blouse was plain, and flowers on her hat.

CASTELLI COLLECTION

1962 #895 "JACQUELINE" models a yellow linen coat with matching sheath dress. Pillbox tulle hat and rhinestone earrings.

COURTESY OF VELVA GEE

1962 #886 "JACQUELINE" in a satin evening gown, long matching stole.

CASTELLI COLLECTION

95

CISSETTE #746 1963 (Bubble cut) Cissette wears a white jersey blouse, lined skirt with matching jacket, and taffeta lace-trimmed panties. A cute white hat, ring and rhinestone earrings. She carries a tag which reads: "I am Cissette and I feel so grown up with my high heeled shoes, nylon hose and lovely clothes. I can walk and sit gracefully because I have jointed knees. You can comb and brush my hair, and Madame Alexander has designed many beautiful outfits for me which you can buy at almost every store." Moving eyes with lashes.

TINKERBELLE (The Magic Fairy) #1110 1969 She is dressed in a shirred one-piece costume equipped with wings. She wears pantyhose and high heeled pumps. A strand of hair, atop her head is tied with a silver bow. Inspired by the movie, "Peter Pan."

10½″ PORTRETTES (1968-1973)

GODEY #1172 1968 Godey has red hair and blue eyes. Five miniature bows and beige lace extend to pink taffeta ruffles. Pink crinoline petticoat, panties, and shoes. Put these all together and they add up to one gorgeous doll.

#1175 1968 RENOIR poses for Pierre Renoir*, while he paints her in a fitted navy blue taffeta dress. A pleated flounce on the bottom of her dress stands out over a crinoline slip. She wears stockings, taffeta panties, and navy blue pumps. A single rose decorates her red hat.

*French painter (1841-1919)

#1171 1969 JENNY LIND PORTRETTE is a beautiful blue-eyed blonde dressed in a long sleeved satin gown. Her taffeta pantaloons and crinoline petticoat are edged in lace.

14" JENNY LIND #1491 1970 Rosettes and lace trim this pink satin formal. Underneath are pink lace trimmed pantaloons and petticoat. Tiny rosebud bouquet.

NOTE: 1969 Jenny Lind's overskirt did not have lace edging, 1970 did.

MELANIE #1173 1970 Tiny pink rosettes adorn this organdy lace gown. She conceals lace trimmed taffeta panties, yellow petticoat and gold shoes.

#1185 1971 SOUTHERN BELLE*
displays an organdy dress with four
rows of lace. A green sash is tied
around her waist. Over her slim
body she wears cotton petticoat and
pantaloons. The wide brimmed hat is
decorated with tulle and tiny flowers.
Around her neck is a gold heart
necklace, her hair styled into two
side buns.

*A beautiful and attractive woman
or girl; a reigning social beauty.

#1186 1972 Elegant describes this
blue-eyed **QUEEN.** Her rich brocade
gown stands out over a crinoline petticoat and taffeta panties. High-
heeled shoes support her silk- stock-
inged legs. For a finishing touch, she
wears a pearl necklace, and a gold
crown set with mock ruby and
rhinestones. Red sash across chest,
wears a crown.

#1180 1973 SCARLETT made this green taffeta dress, jacket, and bonnet from Tara's draperies. She added a crinoline petticoat and pantaloons. Her eyes are green, her hair brunette. She's one-half Irish.

This SCARLETT has blue eyes and dark hair. Her green taffeta dress is trimmed with white braid.

COURTESY OF TERI FROEHLICH

THIS IS THE LISSY SECTION

LISSY (1956-1958)* Lissy made her debut in 1956. She was 11½" tall, all hard plastic, and jointed at the elbows, knees, hips, shoulders, and neck. She was known as the "teenage doll, or Cissy's little sister. She had a small bosom, and slightly high heeled feet. She could be purchased fully dressed or as a basic doll, dressed in a chemise, nylon hose and mules. (slippers)

*1956-1967 Lissy was used for the Little Women. (For Little Women, see separate section.)

1963 Southern Belle, McGuffey Ana, and Scarlett O'Hara were made using the Lissy face.

1966 Cinderella (Lissy face) was sold in a gift box containing the scullery maid and ball gown outfits, or each sold separately.

1967 Laurie (boy from Little Women) was made in Lissy face.

1957 #1142 (yellow) #1152 (yellow-green) These blue-eyed LISSYS attend Sunday School in smartly styled dresses.

Left: Navy blue coat, matching hat, collar and dress. **Center: #1123** 1956-1957. Pink tucked, taffeta dress. **Right #1234** 1956. Pin dot organdy dress with pleated skirt. Wool hat & cardigan, toned to match her dress.

CASTELLI COLLECTION

103

LISSY Organdy dress with matching taffeta panties. Polka dot/flowered pinafore trimmed in purple ric- rac. Flocked net slip. Blonde hair, black eyes.

LISSY AMY - Blonde hair, black eyes. Aqua-blue dress trimmed in lace. Apron straps, white slip and pantaloons are embroidery trimmed. NOTE: See others under Little Women section.

THIS SECTION CONTAINS DOLLS OF COMBINATION VINYL AND PLASTIC.

COURTESY OF CASTELLI COLLECTION

MARYBEL - The doll that gets well (1959-1965) 16" only. "What's that camera man doing in here?" Left: Cotton or nylon shortie pajamas under a lace trimmed robe. Pink slippers. Came in a case with casts, bandages, measle spots, crutches, and etc. Right: One piece pink satin suit.

These two dolls are the same mold. Vinyl head, plastic body, jointed at arms and legs. Swivel waist. Moving eyes with lashes. Rooted, saran hair. Note: Marybel has no ponytail, Edith came with earrings.

EDITH the LONELY DOLL (1958-1959) 16" or 22" Rooted hair in ponytail. Earrings. Taken from Dare Wright's books of Edith and her adventures with bear friends.

106

COURTESY OF CASTELLI COLLECTION

14″ CAROLINE #1312 1962 Riding outfit with cocoa brown pants, lined beige jacket. Underneath she wears a one piece cotton body suit.

12″ BRENDA STARR 1964 135 newspapers across the country published her adventures. She is made entirely different than any other doll. Fully jointed, even at the knees so she can sit gracefully. Golden soft, silky hair can be combed in different arrangements. She came as a basic doll wearing a lace chemise and mules.

A large assortment of clothes were available, including afternoon and evening gowns, beach clothes, sports wear, lingerie, street and at home outfits.

"JANIE" 12" mold (1964-1970) Fully jointed plastic doll with soft vinyl head and arms, moving eyes and lashes, rooted hair. Pigeon- toed. Same body was used for the "Smarty" doll in 1962-3. Used for the following dolls: Janie (1964-1965), Rosy (1969), Michael (1969), Lucinda (1969-1970), Suzy (1970), Gretl, Frederich, Marta (1965-1970) Large Sound of Music dolls.

#1156 1964 Janie is adorable in this organdy dress with bodice of lace and embroidered flowers, and tucked skirt, organdy panties, cotton slip, nylon socks, and tan shoes.

#1135 (1969-1970) LUCINDA Under her long blue taf-feta dress, LUCINDA wears lace and ribbon-trimmed petticoat and pantaloons. Lace-trimmed floral parasol, high buttoned shoes, and a lavishly trimmed hat of rib-bons and feathers, and she is irresistable.

GEORGEANN TINTORI

MARTA, FREDERICH, GRETL, the three pigeon-toed dolls from the Large Sound of Music. (Janie face)

COURTESY OF VELVA GEE

THIS SECTION IS ELISE DOLLS. IT INCLUDES 12″ ELISE (PINKIE, BLUEBOY, ROMEO, JULIET), JOINTED ANKLE ELISE, VINYL HEAD ELISE, AND 17″ ELISE, INCLUDING POLLY AND LESLIE.

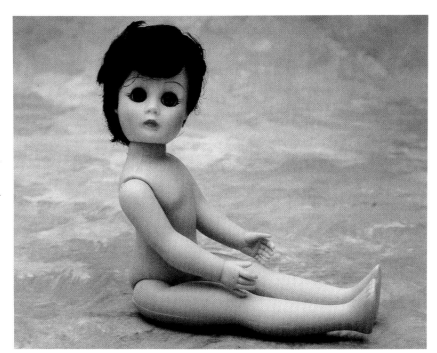

ELISE 12″ all hard plastic body with soft vinyl head. Jointed at the neck, shoulders, and hips. Marked Alexander 1962 on back of neck.

12″ NANCY DREW 1967 Inspired by the mystery books. This white linen sheath dress, matching coat, is accented with green scarf and headband. One of two outfits made.

12″ PINKIE (1975 to date) Doll inspired by Joshua Reynold's (1723-92) painting. Pinkie wears a white sheer dress lined with pink. Her sash matches the ribbon on her poke bonnet. White lace and ribbon trimmed pantaloons. White socks, black shoes.

12″ BLUEBOY (1972 to date) One of the best-known paintings by Thomas Gainsborough (1727-88). Noted for his portraits, and landscapes. Blue Boy wears white cotton shirt with lace trims. Blue jacket, matching britches and hat.

12" LITTLE WOMEN - LAURIE (Elise face)

	Beth	Laurie	Amy	
Jo		Marme		Meg

ROMEO and JULIET (#1360, #1370) 1978 to date. He wears a white cotton shirt, attached to red nylon tights. Contrasting purple jacket with gold/red metalic braid trim. A gem and feather on his hat, brown medieval slippers. Brown hair, blue eyes. She is wearing a long-sleeved chiffon gown over a silk lining. Gold metalic yoke and cap, pearl trimmed. Softly curled brunette hair and blue eyes. Nylons, gold slippers, and ivory lace trimmed pantaloons complete her outfit.

Left: All hard plastic.

Right: Soft vinyl head.

ELISE 1957-1964* Hard plastic body and soft vinyl arms. She is jointed at the knee, hip, shoulder, and neck. She has jointed ankles, so she can wear high heeled shoes. Marked Alexander on back of head. Like Wendy, Cissette, Lissy and Cissy, she could be purchased fully dressed or as a basic doll in chemise, hose and mules. She came in many different outfits; some the same as Cissette and Cissy.

*In 1962-1964, she was made with a vinyl head.

cer
le,
ed
tin

ELISE in an afternoon dress with matching jacket and organdy veiled hat. White taffeta panties, flocked petticoat. Clover shaped earrings and rhinestone brooch.

1962 #1740 Vinyl face **ELISE** has blond hair, blue eyes. Her blue tou tou has a bodice of sequins, which match her tiara. She wears pink panty-hose, satin slippers and tiny rhinestone earrings. Replaced shoes.

PAM TEMPS

BIGGS PUI

ELISE wears a red pleated skirt, knit blouse. Her dainties include a flocked slip and lace- trimmed panties. Who wouldn't want this blue-eyed, brown haired doll in their collection?

COURTESY OF ROSIE ROTHSCHILD

17" ELISE BRIDE (1966 to date) One of different versions.

ELISE (Vinyl) (1966 to date) 17" soft vinyl doll, can be posed in various positions. Black pupiless or blue open/close eyes. Soft, rooted auburn, brunette, or blonde hair. Jointed at the hips, neck, and shoulder. Marked Alexander on back of head. In 1966, she came in four different outfits, the same as Leslie (Negro).

17" ELISE FORMAL #1650 1976 She awaits her date in this lovely styled gown with tulle ruffled yoke and flower trim. A ribbon sash, tied around her waist, flows to the gown hem.

17" 1966-1977 Two versions of ELISE in formals. (See Leslie for third version.)

17" ELISE FORMAL #1755 1967 This delicate blue formal has a pleated skirt, puffed sleeves set with rhinestones and flowers. For jewelry, she wears a sparkling ring, pearl earrings and necklace.

COURTESY OF MARIETTA LANG (SISTER)

17″ 1966 to date Ballerinas came in long or short, pink or blue ballet outfits, but not in both colors every year. All are marked Alexander 1966 on back of head.

META REISTAD

17" ELISE MAGGIE #1720 (1972-1973) Straight hair falls to her waist and touches her short blazer jacket - gold button trim. Her scotch plaid pleated skirt, black pumps, and natural straw hat complete her outfit.

17" PORTRAIT #1780 (1972-1973) ELISE poses for her picture in this full skirted nylon dress, pleated ruffled hem and neckline. Wide brimmed picture hat is trimmed with flowers and lace. Sparkling ring and brooch. Isn't she beautiful?

17" 1965 POLLY has the same moldable body as Elise, although this is referred to as the Polly faced doll.

#1715 1965 POLLY exhibits an apricot striped cotton dress with polka dot ruffled trim over a fluffy slip and panties.

VELVA GEE

17" LESLIE (Polly face) (1965-1971) The same body construction as 17" vinyl Elise. This attractive doll wears a blue lacy formal, pearl necklace. Her dark hair, a cluster of curls on top, is set off with a bow and tiny flowers. 1971

THE FOLLOWING SECTION COVERS 14" DOLLS.

MARY ANN FACE

MARY ANN

MARY ANN 14" (1965 to date)

Fully jointed (neck, shoulders, and hips) doll with soft vinyl head and arms, moving eyes with lashes, rooted hair. Marked Alexander 1966. They sit and stand gracefully.

The following dolls were made from this mold:

Alphabetical order:

Abigal Adams (First Lady/President's wife)

Alice-in-Wonderland (movie released in 1933) - First cloth doll

Bride

Brigetta (Large Sound of Music)

Cinderella — Poor and in gown

Degas (taken from the French painter Degas)

Elizabeth Monroe (First Lady/President's wife)

Gidget (All American Teenager)

Goldilocks

Grandma Jane

Heidi

Jenny Lind (in formal and with cat)

Liesl, Louisa (Large Sound of Music)

Little Granny

Lucinda

Madame Doll (Civil War)

McGuffey Ana (from McGuffey Readers)

Orphan Annie (later Riley's Little Annie)

Peter Pan (from the motion picture)

Rebecca (from the Movie, Rebecca)

Renoir Child, Girl (French painter)

Scarlett (from the book, Gone With the Wind)

Sleeping Beauty

Snow White

Wendy (Walk Disney's movie Peter Pan)

14" ALICE #1552 (1966 to date) Alice has blue eyes, and shoulder length blond hair. White crispy pinafore over a blue cotton dress. Inspired from the book, "Adventures Underground" by Lewis Carrol.

BRIDE #1565* (1973 to date) Lace trimmed bodice and skirt. Tiny white rosebuds held her veil in place. A good-luck garter, nylon stockings, and satin pumps complete her wedding ensemble. What lucky girl will catch the bouquet?

*Came in #1465 and 1570, with only a slight difference in the gown.

CINDERELLA, GOWN #1546 (1970 to date) "Fairy Godmother" dressed Cinderella in this pink and silver net gown, trimmed in rosebuds. Pink crinoline slip, pantaloons, silver slippers, and she's complete for the Ball.

CINDERELLA, POOR #1540 (1966 to date) She wears a cotton dress, apron, and brown shoes. A green kerchief covers her soft blonde hair. She sweeps up the cinders with her straw broom.

DEGAS #1575 (1967 to date) She wears a white organdy flower trimmed duster cap over her long dark hair. Her two tiered cotton dress is accented with a bright pink velvet sash. High buttoned shoes and white stockings cover her feet.

FOR FIRST LADIES, SEE PRESIDENT'S WIVES.

#1520 (1978 to date) GOLDILOCKS chose this blue taffeta dress with overskirt, in which to "visit" the three bears. Her outfit includes velvet vest, eyelet trimmed slip, panties, stockings, and blue pumps. Her golden locks (Goldilocks) are tied back with a black velvet ribbon.

GRANDMA JANE #1420 (1970-1972) Off to visit her grandchildren, is Grandma Jane in this smartly styled shift dress with matching coat. Beige bag and shoes. Glasses, pearl necklace, and earrings.

NOTE: In 1971-1972, Grandma carries a plastic box with wig and rollers. Her dress is lilac blue. Have you visited your Grandma lately?

HEIDI #1480,1580 (1969 to date) Printed cotton dress, embroidered pinafore. Lacy petticoat and panties. White stockings, black shoes and to top it all off, a roller hat.

VELVA GEE

JENNY LIND 14" (1970); 10½" Portrette (1969) These two beauties wear satin formal gowns over lace trimmed petticoats, pantaloons and pink slippers. They carry floral bouquets.

NOTE: 14" doll has lace trimmed neckline and skirt.

JENNY LIND & THE LISTENING CAT #1470 (1970-1971) In a blue cotton dress, Jenny Lind poses with her small cat. Eyelet apron, white stockings and black pumps. A blue ribbon holds back her blonde shoulder length hair.

LITTLE GRANNY #1430 (1966) Pin-dot, lace trimmed dress. One of two versions: other being a floral print.

LUCINDA #1535 (1972 to date) Off to the party in this long pale blue ruffled dress. Ribbon and lace trimmed pantalons and petticoat, suede pumps, trimmed bonnet and a printed parasol.

NOTE: See pigeon-toed Lucinda under the "Janie" section.

14" MADAME DOLL #1460 (1967-1975) Over lace edged pantaloons and slip, she wears a brocade gown trimmed in pink organdy and lace ruffles. Organdy duster cap. Inspired from the book, "Secret of the Madame Doll" by Frances Cavanah.

PAM TEMPS

#1525 (1977 to date) Welcome back **McGUFFEY ANA** in this plaid cotton dress with an organdy pinafore. Field flowers trim her straw picture hat which is worn over her blonde hair in pigtails. White stockings, panties and slip. Black/white high button shoes. Inspired from McGuffey Readers.

PETER PAN #1410 (1969) In conjuction with the motion picture, Madame Alexander dressed Peter Pan in felt leotards, and saw- toothed edged jacket. Matching felt hat, brown belt, soft felt boots. Rooted red hair.

NOTE: See Tinkerbelle under Cissette section.

VELVA GEE COLLECTION

131

PRESIDENT'S WIVES OR FIRST LADIES 14" (1967-1978) Madame Alexander presented these six "First Ladies" to commemorate the 200th birthday of our country. These dolls are plastic and vinly and can sit or stand. Moving eyes with lashes, and individually styled, rooted hair.

MARTHA WASHINGTON #1501 Wife of George Washington (1789-1797) Ivory and gold brocade dress with lace trim. A matching shawl is worn around her shoulders. Lace duster cap partly covers her blonde curls. She carries a brown velvet bag, and wears a pearl necklace.

ABIGAIL ADAMS #1502 Wife of John Adams (1797-1801) Her soft honey blonde hair and brown eyes set off her brocade silk gown. Her lace kerchief is held in place with a sapphire/rhinestone pin. Dainties consist of lace and ribbon trimmed pantaloons and petticoat. Pearl necklace, black shoes.

DOLLY MADISON #1504 Wife of James Madison (1809-1817) A beautiful ivory satin and floral dress with full length matching coat, both trimmed in ivory and silver braid. Her ivory colored headband brings out the brown in her hair and eyes.

MARTHA RANDOLPH #1503 Wife of Thomas Mann Randolph — daughter of Thomas Jefferson (1801-1809) She acted as hostess for her father, President Jefferson, since her mother had died many years before. Her chiffon headband, wrapped around her blonde hair, conceals her top cluster of curls. She wears a tulle lace and ribbon trimmed slip and pantaloons. With pearl necklace, pink pumps, and black crepe cape, she is complete.

133

ELIZABETH MONROE #1505 Wife of James Monroe (1817-1825) This gold and rose brocade dress has lace trimmed three quarter sleeves. The lace collar is adorned with a tiny gold pin. Her elegantly curled hair is pulled up and back, and secured with a jeweled headpiece which matches her pendant necklace.

LOUISA ADAMS #1501 Wife of John Quincy Adams (1825-1829) Lovely blue eyed Louisa Adams is wearing a satin dress with the neckline, sleeves, waist, and hem, all trimmed in tulle and silver glitter braid. Her blonde hair is braided, pulled atop her head, and partially covered with a cluster of curls and rosebuds. White pumps, stockings, and pearl necklace complete her fashion.

REBECCA #1585 (1968 to date) Inspired by the book, Rebecca, later made into a movie. Pin dotted cotton dress, petticoat and panties. Poke bonnet worn over brown braided hair. ⇨

RENOIR GIRL WAS INSPIRED BY THE MASTERPIECES OF THE FRENCH PAINTER PIERRE RENOIR.

⇦

RENOIR GIRL #1476 (1967-1968) Organdy lace trimmed dress, with an added touch of ribbon at the neckline and hem. Natural straw hat trimmed with lace, ribbon, and flowers. High buttoned shoes.

GEORGEANN TINTORI

135

RENOIR GIRL #1477 (1969-1971) She is wearing a white apron with a pink embroidered edging. Under her pink cotton dress she wears a lace trimmed petticoat, long white stockings, and high buttoned shoes. Above her blonde ponytail she wears a straw hat trimmed with ribbon and rosebuds.

RENOIR GIRL #1478 (1972 to date) Lace trimmed organdy dress, with sash at the waist. Pink tafetta petticoat and panties. Organdy poke bonnet w-flower trim. White stockings, pink high button shoes.

NOTE: Earlier ones had straw poke bonnets.

14" SCARLETT #1490 (1968 to date)
Bouffant white organdy, lace trimmed, dress accented with a velvet sash. Tiny green bows in her hair. Nylons and black shoes complete her outfit.

SLEEPING BEAUTY #1595 (1971 to date) Gold taffeta skirt with an overskirt of gold metallic net. Gold braided bodice and tiara.

SNOW WHITE (1967-1976) Made exclusively for Disneyland/World. Snow White wears a blue velveteen bodice attached to a gold taffeta skirt, magenta cape with stand-up collar, crinoline slip, taffeta panties, & black shoes.

SNOW WHITE #1455 (1970 to date) Snow White awaits the Prince in this white tulle gown with rows of satin trim. Covering her shoulders is a silver and white cape with stand-up collar. Satin band in her long dark hair. Silver slippers.

THIS SECTION SHOWS A FEW OF THE 21″ PORTRAIT DOLLS.

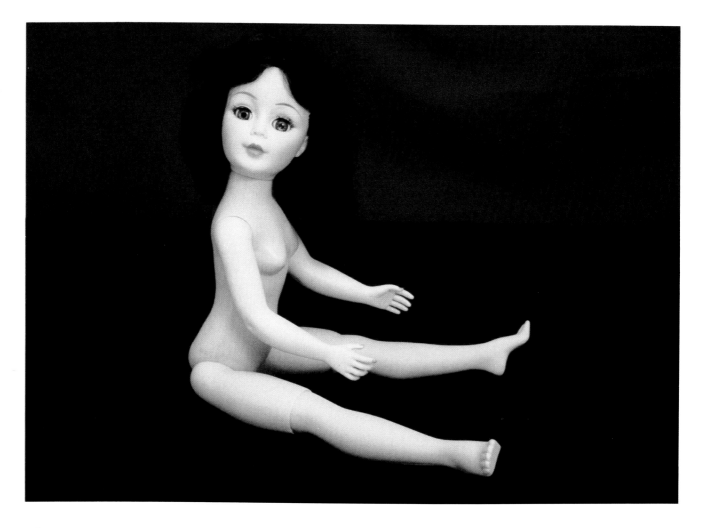

This mold was used for all the 21″ Portrait dolls starting in 1965, with the exception of CoCo dolls in 1966. Same doll as Jacqueline in 1961-1962. **The head is marked Alexander 1961, as are all** the Portrait dolls through the present time. The body is hard plastic and jointed at the **knee,** shoulder, hip, and neck. Vinyl head and arms. Open-close eyes with lashes; blue eye shadow. Blue, green, or brown eyes. Rooted hair.

The following "Ladies" were made from this mold: Agatha, Bride Cornelia, Gainsborough, Godey, Goya, Jenny Lind, Lady Hamilton, Madame Pompadour, Magnolia, Melanie, Mimi, Queen, Renoir, Scarlett, Sourthern Belle.

1966 CoCo dolls are: Godey, Madame Doll, Melanie, Lissy, Renoir, Scarlett.

COURTESY OF MARGE BIGGS, MILLIE FERGUSON — TWIN SISTERS.

SCARLETT (1978); SCARLETT #2210 (1978) Fit for a party is Scarlett, in a rose printed satin gown, accented with a green sash and parasol. Under her large straw hat, trimmed with roses and ribbon, she displays green eyes and brunette hair. Her white petticoat and pantaloons are trimmed in green. She wears an emerald necklace and a ring.

RIGHT: SCARLETT #2174 (1967) Sleeveless green taffeta gown and matching jacket, both garnished in black braid. Gown and jacket sleeves are edged in lace. Her poke bonnet, with flowers and lace, partly hides her long black hair. She wears lace trimmed taffeta panties and nylon hose. Cameo necklace and a ring.

GODEY #2195 (1969) Red velveteen strapless gown with matching coat trimmed in black braid and tiny black buttons. Black hat decorated with six red bows and veil. Blonde hair, blue eyes. Ruby necklace matches her ruby and diamond earrings.

MELANIE #2196 (1970) This truly beautiful doll is dressed in a white dotted swiss dress with three rows of red ribbon woven through lace. Her red parasol matches her red shoes. Brown eyes, brunette hair. Red roses and tiny blue flowers adorn her white hat. Cameo necklace and a sparkling ring.

143

GAINSBOROUGH #2192 (1972) Taken from Thomas Gainsborough, 18th Century painter. Posed for a painting, is this beauty in ecru lace gown over blue taffeta. Three large looped bows give a bustle effect. Straw hat (one side turned up) is adorned with rose buds and tulle. Auburn hair, blue eyes. Pantaloons, crinoline petticoat. Blue shoes. Pearl drop earrings, ring, and heart necklace.

RENOIR #2190 (1973) Soft gold dress with self ruffles on sleeves, bodice and skirt and two deep ruffles on lower front. Sailor hat trimmed with tulle and flowers.

MAGNOLIA #2297 (1977) This lovely auburn haired, blue-eyed beauty is wearing a pink taffeta dress with an inset of 14 rows of lace. Tiny flowers trim her gown and large sheer hat. Pink pantaloons, pink crinoline petticoat are trimmed in lace. Pink shoes. Necklace and ring.

MARIETTA LANG (SISTER)

CORNELIA #2212 (1978) She wears a turquoise blue taffeta gown and matching coat trimmed in silver braid. A large tulle hat with tiny buds, is worn over her blonde hair. Petticoat, pantaloons, nylons and pumps complete her attire. Ring and pearl pendant are her jewelry.

147

SOUND OF MUSIC SECTION

"SOUND OF MUSIC" dolls were made from 1965-1973. They represent the 1959 Broadway Musical written and composed by Oscar Hammerstein and Richard Rodgers. Also famous for such musicals as: Oklahoma (1943), Carousel (1945), South Pacific (1949 Pulitzer Prize), The King and I (1951), and Flower Drum Song (1958). Oscar Hammerstein passed away in 1960.

The "Sound of Music" dolls were made in three different sets. The large sets were made from 1965-1970; the small set 1971-1973.

CASTELLI COLLECTION

The first set of "Sound of Music" used a Lissy doll, two Janie's, two Mary Ann's and a Smarty doll (substitute used for Frederich). Maria (Polly face) came in a brown and white bodice, other sets came in green and white.

SOUND OF MUSIC (1965-1970) (Large Set) 14" LOUISA (Mary Ann face) Green velveteen bodice, white sleeves sewn to a bright pink cotton skirt. Blonde hair in looped braids. White undies, long nylon stockings, black slip on shoes, black eyes. 14" BRIGETTA (Mary Ann face) Front laced weskit worn over a white blouse with eyelet sleeves, red printed skirt. 14" LIESL (Mary Ann face) Pumpkin colored dress, white eyelet sleeves. Striped apron; the bib fastened with two tiny buttons. Straw hat with green braid, and fruit trim. Cocoa brown slip on shoes. The three dolls from the 12"Janie mold are: MARTA — Suspender effect bodice, printed skirt. Long single braid, blue eyes. GRETL — Suede bodice, cotton sleeves, printed skirt. Braided buns, blue eyes. FRIEDRICH — Checked shirt, short suede pants, braid trimmed hat, blonde hair, black eyes. From the Polly mold: MARIA 17" — One piece braid and lace trimmed dress, flowered apron. Straw hat with field flowers.

SOUND OF MUSIC (Small set) 1971-1973 These dolls are hard plastic with the exception of Maria's face, which is vinyl. 8″ dolls are: GRETL — blue printed skirt attached to a red suede top, white puffed sleeves. MARTA — blue eyes, dark brown hair pulled into one back center braid, aqua velveteen, bodice trimmed in braid, organdy sleeves, printed skirt. FREDERICH (FRIEDRICH) — Blue eyes, blonde hair, yellow hat with braid trim, green/white checked shirt, brown suede pants, gold socks, and brown tie shoes. 10½″ dolls from the Cissette mold are: LOUISA with blue eyes, long blonde pigtails. Green velveteen bodice with braid trim and white inset. Printed skirt, black pumps. LIESL, with blonde hair, blue eyes. Orange dress, white eyelet sleeves. Green and white striped apron attached to the bodice with two tiny buttons. Straw hat with fruit and braid trim. Beige pumps. BRIGETTA, Dark hair, brown eyes. Black weskit over white blouse, red printed skirt. Black pumps. MARIA, 12″ Elise doll is a blue-eyed blonde and wears trimmed bodice attached to a green skirt, Flowered apron, and straw hat.

THE FOLLOWING PAGES ARE REDRESSED ALEXANDER DOLLS.

If you have never purchased a doll in "bad shape", fixed her up, and given her a special place in your heart, or collection, then you have missed a wonderful part of the doll world. You don't sew? Then seek someone who can make an outfit for you. (Or write the author.) You can still have the fun of washing, combing and fixing her hair, cleaning her up and adding shoes and socks. Then see if this "orphan" isn't one of your favorite dolls.

This once orphaned Cissette has been given a new home-made gown with matching nightcap. She is thankful she has a good home.

14" Maggie face doll is wearing a pink organdy lace trimmed dress. She asks, "Mother, have you seen my Alexander doll about this big?"

ADOPTED BY GEORGEANN TINTORI

153

Redressed as "Parlor Maid".

ADOPTED BY META REISTAD

1953 One of the very first straight leg Alexander-Kin dolls has been redressed as a ballerina.

154

ADOPTED BY GEORGEANN TINTORI

This group of redressed dolls was made to be loved.

INDEX

SOM = Sound of Music   LW = Little Women   C = Cloth